Hen...
John...ook

Eleanor

this book belongs
to
Henry the 1/8

Henry The 1/8 Joke Book

LEN COLLIS

Illustrated by
STEVEN APPLEBY

DRAGON
GRAFTON BOOKS
A Division of the Collins Publishing Group

LONDON GLASGOW
TORONTO SYDNEY AUCKLAND

Dragon
Grafton Books
A Division of the Collins Publishing Group
8 Grafton Street, London W1X 3LA
Published by Dragon Books 1986
Collection copyright © Len Collis 1986
Illustrations copyright © Steven Appleby
British Library Cataloguing in Publication Data

Henry the ⅛ joke book.
  1. Wit and humor, Juvenile   2. English wit
  and humor
  I.Collis,Len   II. Appleby, Steven
  828′.91402′0809282   PZ7.8

  ISBN 0–583–30932–1

Printed and bound in Great Britain by
Collins, Glasgow
Set in Janson

All rights reserved. No part of this publication may
be reproduced, stored in a retrieval system, or
transmitted, in any form, or by any means, electronic,
mechanical, photocopying, recording or otherwise,
without the prior permission of the publishers.

This book is sold subject to the condition that
it shall not, by way of trade or otherwise, be
lent, re-sold, hired out or otherwise circulated
without the publisher's prior consent in any form of
binding or cover other than that in which it is
published and without a similar condition including
this condition being imposed on the subsequent
purchaser.

Ᵽe Contents

Henry The 1/8 Joke Book

Jokes About Ye Foreign Parts for Ye Telling To Anne Of Cleves

Who ruled Gaul and kept catching colds?
Julius Sneezer.

How was the Roman Empire cut in half?
With a pair of Caesars.

Who entertained Herod with the dance
of the seven sausage skins?
Salami.

What do you call an Indonesian chorus
girl?
A Bali dancer.

What do you call a skinny Apache?
A Red Thindian.

What do you call an Irish Apache?
Tom O'Hawk.

What stands in the middle of Paris and smells nice?
The Eiffel Flower.

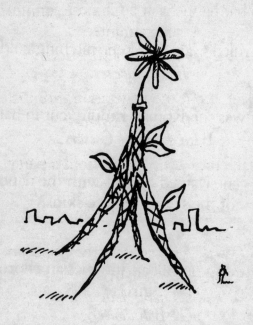

What monster became President of France?
Charles de Ghoul.

What's green, mushy and 2,000 miles long?
The Grape Wall of China.

Where were sausages first cooked?
In Ancient Grease.

What happens at a Chinese cannibal restaurant?
They eat with chap-sticks.

Hear about the vegetarian cannibal?
He only ate Swedes.

What's the best place to hold a party in California?
San Frandisco.

How do you contact the police in Germany?
Dial nein, nein, nein.

How do you contact the police in Australia?
Dial 666.

What do you call an Eskimo wearing 12
balaclava hats?
Anything you like – he won't hear you.

What do you call an Alaskan cow?
An Eskimoo.

What money do Eskimos use?
Ice lolly.

How does an Eskimo build a house?
Igloos it together.

Hear about the Eskimo who ate a candle?
He wanted some light refreshment.

What makes the Tower of Piza lean?
It won't eat much.

What's tall and wobbly and stands in the middle of Paris?
The Trifle Tower.

What's a fjord?
A Norwegian motor car.

A few Quick Jokes for Ye Telling To Anne Boleyn

What's grey, spotty and weighs two tons?
A hippo with measles.

What happens when snails have a fight?
They slug it out.

How do snails get their shells shiny?
They use snail varnish.

Where do baby beans come from?
The stalk brings them.

Where would you find a queue of bees?
At a buzz stop.

What goes crunk-crick?
The seatbelt of a Japanese car.

Hear about the car with a wooden engine
and wooden wheels?
It wooden go.

What did the scoutmaster say when his
car horn was mended?
Beep repaired.

What's a mermaid?
A deep-she fish.

Hear about the mad robot?
He had a screw loose.

Why don't robots ever panic?
They have nerves of steel.

What's big, green and wrinkled?
An unripe elephant.

What crawls along going ding-dong,
ding-dong?
A wounded Avon lady.

What's the best way to see a flying
saucer?
Trip up a waitress.

Why are weathercocks conceited?
They're all vane creatures.

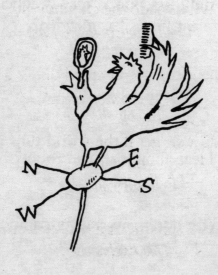

What are round, green and smell fishy?
Brussels sprats.

What's a road-hog?
A pig-headed driver.

Who does Dracula go out with?
His girl-fiend.

What did one rock pool say to the other rock pool?
"Show us your mussels".

What made the chimney ill?
It had a touch of the flue.

What happens if you crawl under a cow?
You get a pat on the head.

What do you get if the world runs out of olive oil?
Rusty olives.

Who's in charge at a hankie factory?
The hankie chief.

Hear about the flood at the detergent factory?
The walls caved in with a thickening sud.

Hear about the watch factory that closed down?
They wound up the business.

What do you have to know to be an auctioneer?
Lots.

Do litter collectors have to be trained?
No – they pick it up as they go along.

What's the best dog to have in your kitchen?
A cooker spaniel.

When do mountaineers retire?
When they're past their peak.

Hear about the sword-swallower who resigned?
He was fed up to the hilt with his job.

What do you call the place where an optician has a shop?
A site for sore eyes.

What happens if you plug the electric blanket into the toaster?
You keep popping out of bed.

What sits in a tree waiting to be exchanged for a meal?
A luncheon vulture.

What happens at a cannibal wedding?
They toast the bride.

What happened when the lady ghost met the man ghost?
It was love at first fright.

Where do you find a vampire at 11 a.m.?
Taking a coffin break.

Who shouted "Knickers!" at the big bad wolf?
Little Rude Riding Hood.

Jokes About Fairies And Witches for Telling To Ye Young Princess Elizabeth

Why do witches ride broomsticks?
Vacuum cleaners are too heavy.

Where do witches learn to fly
broomsticks?
At demon-strations.

How do witches get slim enough to ride broomsticks?
They go to Weight Witches.

What do witches use for racing?
Vroomsticks.

What happens when witches run out of magic potions?
They go abroad for a spell.

Who flies over beaches on a broomstick?
A sandwich.

How does a witch tell the time?
She wears a witch watch.

Why do witches keep skunks?
To make magic smells.

Why is it better to be a Fairy Queen?
You can have anything you wand.

What do you get if you cross a witch
with an ice cube?
A cold spell.

Witch: Do fairies have names?
Fairy: Of course. My name is Nuff.
Witch: I've never come across that name
       before.
Fairy: Surely everyone's heard of *Fairy
       Nuff?*

What would you call a boat captained by
Tinkerbell?
A pantomime ferry.

What do pixies learn at school?
The elfabet.

What do pixies have for tea?
Fairy cakes.

What happens if you sleep with your
head under the pillow?
The fairies take all your teeth away.

What do you call a magician in a
spaceship?
A flying sorceror.

What's six and Grumpy?
The Seven Dwarfs.

Who wrote jokes and never grew up?
Peter Pun.

Why did Cinderella get shown a yellow
card at the football match?
She went in late for the ball.

Doctor, doctor, I feel like a witch.
What you need is a spell in hospital.

Jokes About Ye Funny Names for Telling To Ye Mistress Seymour

What do you call a man carrying a spear?
Lance.

What do you call a man carrying ten
spears?
Lancelot.

What do you call a man with a stick tied
to his leg?
Rodney.

What do you call a woman disappearing
over the horizon?
Dot.

What do you call a woman who throws
her bills on the fire?
Bernadette.

What do you call a man wearing a raincoat?
Mac.

What do you call a man wearing TWO raincoats?
Max.

What do you call a woman with a broken shoe?
Lucille.

What do you call a girl carrying an oven?
Anita.

What do you call a girl spreading a slice of bread?
Marge.

What do you call a girl carrying a mower?
Lorna.

What do you call a girl carrying a Union Jack?
Britt.

What do you call a man carrying a vase?
Ern.

What do you call a man carrying
binoculars?
Seymour.

What do you call a girl climbing up a
wall?
Ivy.

What do you call a man with a wooden
head?
Edward.

What do you call a man with three
wooden heads?
Edward Woodward.

What do you call a man down on his
knees?
Neil.

What do you call a man digging up a
bog?
Pete.

What do you call a man carrying a
spade?
Doug.

What do you call a man carrying half a
spade?
Douglas.

What do you call a man carrying a
forged fiver?
Dud.

What do you call a girl standing between
two goalposts?
Annette.

What do you call a man carrying a
haystack?
Rick.

What do you call a woman juggling beer
bottles?
Beatrix.

What do you call a woman juggling beer
bottles and a snooker cue?
Beatrix Potter.

What do you call a boy carrying a
carpet?
Matt.

What do you call a man carrying a
number plate?
Reg.

What do you call a woman carrying two
sheets of glass?
Patty O'Doors.

What do you call a woman with one leg
shorter than the other?
Eileen.

What do you call a man with scratches
on him?
Claude.

What do you call a girl with a tent tied to
her foot?
Peg.

What do you call a man with two
smashed-up cars?
Rex.

What do you call a man wrapped in
newspaper?
Russell.

What do you call a man who has fallen
into the sea and can't swim?
Bob.

What do you call a man hanging from
the ceiling with a light bulb in his
mouth?
Sean de Lear.

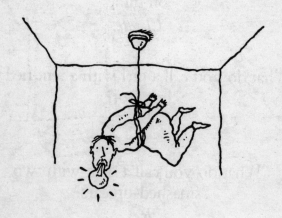

Knock-Knocks for Ye Amusement Of Catherine Howard

Knock! Knock!
Who's there?
Diploma.
Diploma who?
Diploma to mend de burst pipe.

Knock! Knock!
Who's there?
Israeli.
Israeli who?
Israeli great to see you again.

Knock! Knock!
Who's there?
Diesel.
Diesel who?
Diesel make you laugh.

Knock! Knock!
Who's there?
Norma Lee.
Norma Lee who?
Norma Lee we go fishing on Sunday.

Knock! Knock!
Who's there?
Estelle.
Estelle who?
Estelle raining out here.

Knock! Knock!
Who's there?
Jaws.
Jaws who?
Jaws one Cornetto...

Knock! Knock!
Who's there?
Irish stew.
Irish stew who?
Irish stew in the name of the law.

Knock! Knock!
Who's there?
Mandalay.
Mandalay who?
Mandalay the new carpet.

Knock! Knock!
Who's there?
Desdemona.
Desdemona who?
Desdemona I owe you.

Knock! Knock!
Who's there?
Horse Fair.
Horse Fair who?
Horse Fair in love and war.

Knock! Knock!
Who's there?
Nicholas.
Nicholas who?
Nicholas girls shouldn't climb ladders.

Knock! Knock!
Who's there?
Miniature.
Miniature who?
Miniature ready we can go.

Knock! Knock!
Who's there?
Rufus.
Rufus who?
Rufus collapsing so come out quick!

Knock! Knock!
Who's there?
Senior.
Senior who?
Senior light on – can I come in?

Knock! Knock!
Who's there?
Walrus.
Walrus who?
Walrus asking silly questions, you are.

Knock! Knock!
Who's there?
Mayonnaise.
Mayonnaise who?
Mayonnaise have seen the glory of the
    coming of the Lord...

Knock! Knock!
Who's there?
Candy.
Candy who?
Candy gasman come in to read de meter?

Knock! Knock!
Who's there?
Mustapha.
Mustapha who?
Mustapha word with you.

Knock! Knock!
Who's there?
Handel.
Handel who?
Handel your cash over, this is a hold-up.

Knock! Knock!
Who's there?
Dishwasher.
Dishwasher who?
Dishwasher the way I talked when I lost
  my false teeth.

Knock! Knock!
Who's there?
Sofa.
Sofa who?
Sofa once do as you're told!

Knock! Knock!
Who's there?
Sonia.
Sonia who?
Sonia foot, I can smell it from here.

Knock! Knock!
Who's there?
Armageddon.
Armageddon who?
Armageddon outa here!

Knock! Knock!
Who's there?
Monica.
Monica who?
Monica elastic has broken so let me in
    quick!

Knock! Knock!
Who's there?
Amanda.
Amanda who?
Amanda mend the telly.

Knock! Knock!
Who's there?
Asia.
Asia who?
Asia wish you'd open this door.

Knock! Knock!
Who's there?
Europe.
Europe who?
Europe early this morning.

Knock! Knock!
Who's there?
Oil Sheikh.
Oil Sheikh who?
Oil Sheikh hands with you before I go.

Knock! Knock!
Who's there?
2p.
2p who?
2p or not 2p, that is the question...

Knock! Knock!
Who's there?
Delia.
Delia who?
Delia cards right and I might let you take
  me out!

Musical Jokes
for Ye Telling
To Catherine Parr

Who sat on crates in a train and wrote
music?
Luggage van Beethoven.

Why did the composer spend all his
money?
He was on a Chopin spree.

How did the concert pianist feel when he
lost his music?
Liszt-less.

Hear about the burglar who broke into a
music shop?
He got away with the lute.

Who sings, dances and cleans windows?
Shammy Davis Jnr.

Where can you get a job playing a
rubber trumpet?
In an elastic band.

Who sings at big hotels?
Hilton John.

What do South Pacific fish sing?
"Salmon chanted evening..."

What musical instrument do Spanish
fishermen play?
Cast-a-nets.

What singing birds come from
Cornwall?
The Parrots of Penzance.

Who's top of the South American charts?
Bolivia Newton-John.

What do you call a swinging sweet?
Simon le bon bon.

Where's the best place to weigh a pie?
"Somewhere over the rainbow, weigh a pie…"

Who sang White Christmas and exploded?
Bang Crosby.

What do you call five bottles of lemonade?
A pop group.

What pop star zooms along the motorway at 100 mph?
Mick Jaguar.

Who lives in the desert and invented jive?
Sheikh Rattle 'n Roll.

What music do ghosts listen to?
James Ghoulway.

What's a harp?
A nude piano.

What do you get if you cross a grizzly with a harp?
A bear-faced lyre.

How do fish get their pianos to sound right?
They call in the piano tuna.

How do you get musical water?
Make it piping hot.

What's hot and goes pop in the oven?
Bakin' Stevens.

What do football fans sing at Christmas?
"Yule never walk alone..."

What do gorillas sing at Christmas?
"Jungle bells, jungle bells..."

What did Noah sing at Christmas?
"'Ark the herald angels sing..."

What do sailors sing at Christmas?
"Yule Britannia…"

What does Mrs. B. White sing at Christmas?
"And may all your Chris … Mrs. B. White."

What do slimmers sing at Chrismas?
"A weigh in a manger…"

Goode Olde Jokes for Ye Telling To Cardinal Wolsey

What happened to Boadicea when she
lost the battle?
Julius seized 'er.

Who was the greatest entertainer in
biblical times?
Samson. He brought the house down.

Who invented fireplaces?
Alfred the Grate.

Who invented chiropody?
William the Corncurer.

Who lost at Waterloo and exploded?
Napoleon Blownapart.

What did they call Mothering Sunday in
ancient Egypt?
Mummy's Day.

How did the ancient Egyptians get
about?
By pharaohplane.

What did King Arthur say to the
Knights of the Round Table?
"Don't just sit there – slay something".

Who sailed round Ireland and invented
mints?
Marc O'Polo.

What did Adam do when he wanted
some sugar?
Raised Cain.

Who led hordes of fighting convent
girls?
Attila the Nun.

Why do nuns always wear black?
It's a habit they get into.

Where did the Vikings drink?
At Norse troughs.

What mechanical man saved Scotland?
Robot the Bruce.

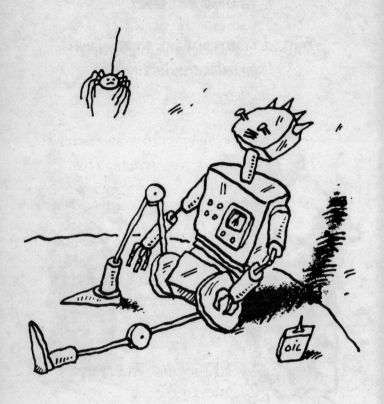

What made Lady Godiva ride in the nude?
She had nothing else on at the time.

Who were the world's smallest
sweethearts?
Gnomeo and Juliet.

Who rode a camel and blew up the
Magic Roundabout?
Florence of Arabia.

How do they serve eggs in a monastery?
Out of the frying pan, into the friar.

Where's Yarmouth?
Under yar nose.

Who painted the Mona Lisa and
invented fizzy drinks?
Lemonado da Vinci.

How do Red Indians send secret
messages?
They use smokeless fuel.

What's a Hindu?
Lays eggs.

When does a vicar walk on his hands?
On Palm Sunday.

What did Noah do when it got dark?
He turned on the flood lights.

What did they call Julius Caesar on a
foggy night in Scotland?
A Roman in the gloamin'.

Jokes About Ye Doctors And Patients for Telling To Ye Queen Catherine Of Aragon

Doctor, doctor, I feel like a Rawlplug.
Yes, I can see you're all screwed up.

Doctor, doctor, I hide under the bed all
day.
You must be a little potty.

Doctor, doctor, I think parts of me are becoming invisible.

Yes – I can see you're not all there.

Doctor, doctor, I'm at death's door.

Don't worry – I'll pull you through.

Doctor, doctor, I have this nightmare where I'm acting at a theatre, and I fall down a trapdoor.

It's just a stage you're going through.

Doctor, doctor, I feel like a toilet.

I can see you're looking a bit flushed.

Doctor, doctor, people keep ignoring me.
Next please.

Doctor, doctor, I feel like a snail.
You need bringing out of your shell.

Doctor, doctor, my mother can't stop
stealing things, and neither can I.
I can see you take after her.

Doctor, doctor, I feel like a wardrobe.
What's got into you?
Two jackets and a suit.

Doctor, doctor, I keep thinking my name is Fred.
I'd prefer you to be frank with me.

Doctor, doctor, I've swallowed a spoon.
Well, sit there and don't stir.

Doctor, doctor, can you help me out?
Certainly – which way did you come in?

Doctor, doctor, I have only 59 seconds to live.
Hang on a minute.

Doctor, doctor, it hurts when I do this.
Well, don't do it then.

Doctor, doctor, I feel like a pound note.
Go out shopping – the change will do you good.

Doctor, doctor, I keep seeing spots before my eyes.
Have you seen a specialist?
No – just spots.

Doctor, doctor, I've swallowed the bedside clock.
Now don't alarm yourself.

Doctor, doctor, I feel like a duck-doo.
What's a duck-doo?
It goes quack, quack.

Doctor, doctor, will you cure my spots?
I can't make rash promises.

Doctor, doctor, I get this feeling that I'm covered in gold paint.
Don't worry – it's just a gilt complex.

Doctor, doctor, I feel like a watch.
Just hang on a tick.

Doctor, doctor, I see this spinning insect all the time.
Don't worry – it's just a bug that's going round.

Doctor, doctor, I've just swallowed a bone.
Are you choking?
No, I'm serious.

Doctor, doctor, I'm terrified of travelling by air.
I can assure you your fears are groundless.

Doctor, doctor, I've just eaten a pencil –
what shall I do?
Use a pen.

Doctor, doctor, I keep imagining I'm
trapped on a beach with the sea coming
in.
I'll give you something to tide you over.

Doctor, doctor, I keep thinking I'm a
bucket.
Yes – you look a little pail.

Doctor, doctor, I'm frightened I'll be snatched up by a giant bird.
You mustn't let yourself get carried away.

Doctor, doctor, I'm having trouble with my breathing.
We'll soon put a stop to that.

Receptionist: Doctor, the Invisible Man is here.
Tell him I can't see him now.

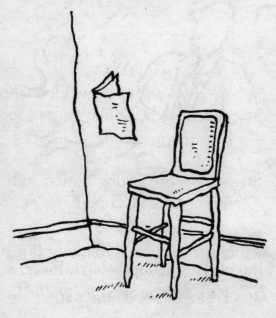

Jokes About Knaves, Dum-dums, Varlets And Wallies for Telling To Ye Ladies-in-waiting And Other Wenches

Hear about the wally with a video who taped programmes he didn't want to see?
He played them when he was out.

Who went to the wrong station and never became famous?
Waterloo Bear.

Hear about the dopey hitch-hiker?
He got up early to avoid the traffic.

Who didn't fly first?
The Wrong Brothers.

How do you say "idiot" in French?
Lagoon

Hear about the village idiot who went to
the dentist?
He wanted a wisdom tooth put in.

Hear about the crook who broke his leg?
He fell off the back of a lorry.

How do you spot the nitwit on an oil
rig?
He's the one feeding bread to the helicopters.

What's written on turf used by dumbo lawn-layers?
"Green side up".

How do you get a one-armed fool out of a tree?
Wave to him.

Hear about the stupid tug-of-war team?
They were disqualified for pushing.

Hear about the man who stole some rhubarb?
He was put into custardy.

What do you call a fly in an idiot's ear?
A space invader.

Hear about the glassblower who sucked instead of blowing?
He got a pane in his stomach.

What do you call a wally riding a bike?
A dope pedlar.

Hear about the village idiot who changed his mind?

It still didn't work.

Hear about the three wallies firing shots in the air?
One missed.

Hear about the nutty football team manager who flooded the pitch?
He wanted to bring on his sub.

What do you get if you cross a dum-dum with a frozen drink?
A wallypop.

Why did the crook saw the legs off his bed?
He wanted to lie low for a while.

Do you know why the halfwit returned his pool table to the factory?
He said the water leaked through the pockets.

Hear about the bank robber who sent the money back?
He was generous to a vault.

Hear about the crackpot who drove his car into a river?
He wanted to dip the headlights.

A policeman spotted an old man in the street dragging a brick on a lead.

The policeman said: "I see you're taking your – er, dog for a walk." The old man looked blank. "No, I'm not," he said, "I'm dragging this brick along."

"That's all right then," said the policeman. "I thought you might be imagining things."

When he was out of earshot, the old man picked up the brick and whispered: "That fooled him, didn't it, Rover?"

What happens if your friends are lunatics?
You'll find they're all crazy about you.

How do you spot an idiot in a car-wash?
He's the one on a motorbike.

Hear about the stupid motorist who couldn't find the M6?
He went up the M3 twice.

Hear about the idiot who hurt himself raking up leaves?
He fell out of the tree.

Jokes for All Seasons for Ye Telling To Sir Thomas More

How do misers keep warm when it's cold?

They sit round a candle.

How do misers keep warm when it's VERY cold?

They light it.

Hear about the man who stayed up all night working out where the sun had gone?

Next morning it dawned on him.

Hear about the man who was badly sunburned?

He got what he was basking for.

What do skeletons do when it rains?
Get wet.

What happened to the man who stole a
calendar?
He got twelve months.

Hear about the man who was drenched
in beer?
He got caught in an ale storm.

Was he pleased about it?
No – he felt bitter.

Ye School Jokes for Telling To Ye Young Prince Edward

Hear about the school run by a one-eyed headmaster?
He has a vacancy for another pupil.

How do you raise the level of teaching?
Use upstairs classrooms.

What's a bwain?
Something bwight kids have.

What's red and good at sums?
A strawberry with a calculator.

What exams do gardeners take?
Hoe levels.

Hear about the teacher who swallowed a dictionary?
He was lost for words.

What's a forum?
Two-um plus two-um.

Who sets fire to classrooms?
The school blazer.

Teacher: What's an icon?
Boy: It's what an oak tree grows from.

When do chickens come out from school?
At four o'cluck.

Hear about the boy who spilt glue over his maths book?
He got stuck in the middle of a sum.

Hear about the flea who failed his exams?
His work wasn't up to scratch.

Teacher: Who gave you that black eye?
Boy: Nobody – I fought for it.

Where do they cook school dinners?
In a mushroom.

Who runs the school disco?
A desk jockey.

Hear about the boy who went to bed
with a ruler?
He wanted to see how long he slept.

Student: Does this pen write under
water?
Shop assistant: Yes – and other words too.

Hear about the teacher who wore dark
glasses?
He had a very bright class.

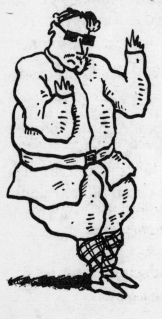

Why can't cross-eyed teachers get any work done?
They can't control their pupils.

Hear about the boy who took a car to school?
He drove his teacher up the wall.

Where do cannibals go to school?
Eton.

Teacher on telephone: Mrs Jones, your son has swallowed a 50p piece.
Mrs Jones: That's okay, it's his dinner money.

Did you hear about the Indian chief with three wives? He reckoned his favourite wife was worth both the others put together – so when he came to refurnish the wigwam he got cheap buffalo skins for those two, and splashed out on a luxury hippopotamus skin for his favourite.
Which proves that the squaw on the hippopotamus is equal to the sum of the squaws on the other two hides!

Ye Riddles And Ye Rib-ticklers Suitable for Ye Princess Mary

What's yellow and wears a mask?
The lone lemon.

What sits in a fruit bowl and shouts for help?
A damson in distress.

What's brown, wrinkled and drinks from the wrong side of the glass?
A prune with hiccups.

Hear about the lioness who got towed away?
She parked on a yellow lion.

What do you call an Irish spider?
Paddy Longlegs.

What do you call an Irish author?
A writing pad.

How do you make anti-freeze?
Hide her nightie.

What happens when fat people step on
the bathroom scales?
They get shown up in a big weigh.

What has two tails, three trunks and five
legs?
An elephant with spare parts.

What did the butler say as he handed his master the cheese biscuits?
"Your crackers, m'lord."

Who lived in a house with two bathrooms, and painted Can-Can girls?
Two Loos Lautrec.

What do you call a Scottish farmer who makes his son polish shoes?
McKay – while the son shines.

Hear about the boy magician who was practising sawing his sister in half?
She's in hospital – wards 1 and 2.

What happens if you read a first-aid book?
You'll meet with a chapter of accidents.

What do you call a boomerang that doesn't come back?
A stick.

Why don't cats shave?
Because 8 out of 10 prefer Whiskers.

Hear about the dog who limped into a
Wild West saloon with a bandage round
his foot?
*He said: I'm looking for the critter who shot
my paw.*

Hear about the football manager who
signed up a matchstick?
*He needed a striker to work from the edge of
the box.*

Why did the chicken run on to the
football pitch?
The referee whistled for a fowl.

Why did the hedgehog cross the road?
To see his flatmate.

What happened to the yacht that
overturned in shark infested waters?
It came back with a skeleton crew.

Hear about the world's worst athlete?
He ran a bath and came second.

Hear about the dizzy Boy Scout?
He spent all day doing good turns.

Hear about the short-sighted harpoonist?
He won the Miss Whales competition.

Hear about the boy who was christened
Six and Seven Eighths?
His dad picked the name out of a hat.

What made the bald man buy another
wig?
He felt a change of 'air would do him good.

What's brown and sticky and comes at
you from all directions?
Stereophonic toffee.

What do you get if you pull your
underpants up to your neck?
A chest of drawers.

What happened to the couple who hated each other, and went to make a wish at the wishing well?

They both fell in.

Books for Ye Recommended Reading

SKINNY GIANT *by Talbot Thynne*

JELLY FOR TEA *by Eileen Joyit*

THE TWO OF US *by Ewan Mee*

BREAKFAST TIME *by Chris P. Bacon*

GIVE IT 'ERE *by Les Avitt*

THE BISCUIT EATER *by Martin Zempty*

END OF A LONG DAY *by Gladys Over*

DON'T WAKE THE BABY *by Elsie Cries*

A POLICEWOMAN'S LOT *by Sheila Restew*

GREETINGS! *by L. O. Friend*

HEAR, HEAR *by Liz N. Toomey*

CONTINENTAL BREAKFAST *by Roland Butter*

HOT HEAD *by Aaron Fire*

LAZY DOG *by Eliza Sleep*

DESPERATE SPINSTER *by Mary Mee*

LOST IN LONDON *by Wanda Round*

TUG OF WAR *by Eve Hoe*

THE POWER OF BINOCULARS *by Seymour Withem*

SHOES FOR REPAIR *by Lucille Ansole*

DON'T HURT ME *by I. Bruce Easily*

ARITHMETIC SIMPLIFIED *by Lois Carmen Denominator*

DEFENDING AT FOOTBALL *by Mark A. Mann*

TRUE OR FALSE? *by Adam Gessin*

MOT FAILURE *by Russ T. Chassy*

AUCTIONEERING *by Arthur N. E. Morbids*

THE RAG AND BONE MAN *by Laurie Lodajunk*

LUNCHTIME SNACK *by V. Landham Pye*

IS THAT THE PHONE? *by Isabel Ringing*

HUNGRY CANNIBAL *by Henrietta Mann*

MY HAPPIEST DAY *by Trudy Light*

SPARE PARTS *by Justin Case*

DON'T SIT DOWN *by Stan Dupright*

CHANNEL ONE *by Bebe See*

FOUND OUT *by Hugh R. Introuble*

AFTER THE MARATHON *by I. M. Aitken*

NO MERCY *by Ruth Less*

DESERT CROSSING *by I. Rhoda Camel*

SHORT BREAK *by T. N. Biscuits*

CHAMBERMAID'S JOB *by Carrie Potts*

GET RICH QUICK *by W. Money*

ENGLAND FOREVER *by Ruby Tanya*

DESPERATE SMOKER *by Mustapha Fagg*

PASS THE TOWEL *by Hans Wet*

THE HOLD-UP *by Andy Tover*

cracked egg
by Michelle Broke

THEY KNOW WE'RE COMING *by Millicent Cable*

CANDID CONVERSATION *by Frank and Ernest Lee*

BE SERIOUS *by Jo Kover*

HOLD YOUR SKIRT *by Winn D. Day*

STONY BROKE *by M. T. Pockets*

GENUINE PREDICTIONS *by Mark Myword*

MY WELL-BEHAVED BOYFRIEND *by I. Doris Manners*

GRETNA GREEN *by Marion Secret*

PS *by Adeline Extra*

STAN LAUREL *by Olive Veradi*

HOLIDAY SPOT *by Isla Wight*

LIFE ON AN INDIAN RESERVATION *by T. P. Dweller*

BAD MEMORY *by Ivor Gott*

BBC IS BORING *by Watson Otherside*

I'M IN TROUBLE *by C. Lee Boy*

SPANISH GREED *by Juan Toomani*

SWEDISH LION CUBS *by Bjorn Free*

DICTATOR'S DREAM *by F. Harold Theworld*

EMPTY CLASSROOM *by Wendy Bellgoes*

BURIED TREASURE *by Doug Itup*

LOOKING AFTER BABIES *by Kieran Love*

Jokes for Ye King's Own Amusement

Brother: You've just reversed your car
    over my bike.
Sister: It's your own fault – you
    shouldn't leave it in the hall.

Dr Watson: Holmes, why is that door
    painted yellow?
Sherlock Holmes: It's a-lemon-entry, my
    dear Watson.

Patient: I'm pleased the x-rays show I'm
    normal, doctor.
Doctor: Indeed yes – both of your heads
    are perfectly OK.

Girl: You need to be a good singer in our
    house.
Friend: Why's that?
Girl: The lock on the loo door is broken.

Policeman: Sir, your wife fell out of your
car a mile back.
Driver: That's a relief – I thought I'd
gone deaf.

Boy: Mummy, what's a werewolf?
Mother: Be quiet and comb your face.

Cannibal wife: I don't know what to
make of my husband these
days.
Friend: I'll lend you my recipe book.

Our cat is great at catching mice. He eats
lumps of cheese, then waits by the
mousehole with baited breath.

Baby sardine: Mummy, what's a
submarine?
Mother sardine: It's just a tin of people.

First stork: Why are you standing on one
leg?
Second stork: Because you just trod on the
other one.

Motorist: I got a new car for my wife
yesterday.
Friend: That sounds like a good swap.

Waiter: Everything's on the menu, sir.
Customer: So I see – could you bring me
a clean one?

Customer: Waiter, what's this beetle doing
in my soup?
Waiter: The fly's on holiday, sir.

Customer: Waiter, will my omelette be
long?
Waiter: No sir – round.

Customer: Waiter, why are there TWO
flies in my soup?
Waiter: It's a special offer, sir.

Customer: Waiter, have you any sauce?
Waiter: Yes sir – HP.
Customer: No, I'll pay cash.

Joke Books

Markoe and Phillips

Nutty Knock Knocks — 80p ☐

Joseph Heck

Dinosaur Riddle Book — £1.25 ☐

Bill Howard

The Saturday Starship Joke Book — £1.25 ☐

Deborah Manley

The Encyclopedia of Jokes — £1.50 ☐

Verse and Rhyme

Jennifer Mulherin (ed)

Old Fashioned Nursery Rhymes — £1.25 ☐

Puzzle Books and Quiz Books

Ronald Ridout

Picture Words — 95p ☐
Word Hunt — 75p ☐
In Other Words — 75p ☐
My Word — 95p ☐
Word for Word — 75p ☐
First Puzzles — 75p ☐
Konky Puzzles — 75p ☐
Puzzles Galore — 75p ☐
More Puzzles — 75p ☐
Top Puzzles — 95p ☐
What's the Word — 95p ☐
Clever Crosswords Book 1 — 95p ☐
Clever Crosswords Book 2 — 95p ☐
Clever Crosswords Book 3 — 95p ☐
Clever Crosswords Book 4 — 95p ☐

Children's Britannica

Children's Britannica Quiz Book — £1.25 ☐
Children's Britannica Nature Quiz Book — £1.25 ☐
Children's Britannica History Quiz Book — £1.25 ☐

To order direct from the publisher just tick the titles you want
and fill in the order form.

Fiction in paperback from Dragon Books

Mr T	£1.50	☐
Ann Jungman		
Vlad the Drac	£1.25	☐
Vlad the Drac Returns	£1.25	☐
Vlad the Drac Superstar	£1.50	☐
Jane Holiday		
Gruesome and Bloodsocks	£1.25	☐
Thomas Meehan		
Annie	£1.50	☐
Michael Denton		
Eggbox Brontosaurus	£1.25	☐
Glitter City	£1.25	☐
Fantastic	£1.25	☐
Marika Hanbury Tenison		
The Princess and the Unicorn	£1.25	☐
Alan Davidson		
A Friend Like Annabel	£1.25	☐
Just Like Annabel	£1.25	☐
Maureen Spurgeon		
BMX Bikers	£1.50	☐
BMX Bikers and the Dirt-Track Racers	£1.50	☐
T R Burch		
Ben and Blackbeard	£1.25	☐
Ben on Cole's Hill	£1.25	☐
Jonathan Rumbold		
The Adventures of Niko	£1.25	☐
Marcus Crouch		
The Ivory City	95p	☐
Lynne Reid Banks		
The Indian in the Cupboard	£1.50	☐
Nina Beachcroft		
A Spell of Sleep	£1.25	☐
Cold Christmas	£1.50	☐
Graham Marks		
The Finding of Stoby Binder	£1.50	☐
David Osborn		
Jessica and the Crocodile Knight	£1.50	☐

To order direct from the publisher just tick the titles you want
and fill in the order form.

All these books are available at your local bookshop or newsagent, or can be ordered direct from the publisher.

To order direct from the publishers just tick the titles you want and fill in the form below.

Name _____

Address _____

_____

Send to:
Dragon Cash Sales
PO Box 11, Falmouth, Cornwall TR10 9EN.

Please enclose remittance to the value of the cover price plus:

UK 45p for the first book, 20p for the second book plus 14p per copy for each additional book ordered to a maximum charge of £1.63.

BFPO and Eire 45p for the first book, 20p for the second book plus 14p per copy for the next 7 books, thereafter 8p per book.

Overseas 75p for the first book and 21p for each additional book.

Dragon Books reserve the right to show new retail prices on covers, which may differ from those previously advertised in the text or elsewhere.